Tawashis
in Crochet™

General Information

Many of the products used in this pattern book can be purchased from local craft, fabric and variety stores, or from the Annie's Attic Needlecraft Catalog (see Customer Service information on page 32).

Contents

Introduction

According to Wikipedia, "The tawashi (a bundle) is a Japanese traditional scrubbing brush to wash off the dirt. The typical tawashi is Kamenoko Tawashi."

"An acrylic tawashi (akuriru tawashi) is a tawashi made of acrylic [yarn], typically knitted or crocheted."

Tawashi scrubbers have been used in Japan for about 25 years, but have only recently found their way to the United States. In Japan, the yarn normally used to make tawashi has anti-bacterial qualities, but, unfortunately, this yarn isn't readily available in the United States yet. Tawashi are both cute and very quick to make. Because they are so cute, tawashi are a great tool to use to encourage children to help with cleaning chores.

There are three different styles of tawashi included in this book. These styles include the following: the mitt scrubber into which you slip your hand, the flat scrubber that you use like a rag, and the roll-shaped tube scrubbers that are more like a traditional scrubber.

A basket of tawashi and a bottle of earth-friendly dish soap or bath soap would make a wonderful gift.

Tawashi made in acrylic yarns are flexible and maintain their shape and color after lots of usage. Tawashi can also be made from cotton yarn or a yarn made from a combination of fibers.

Tawashi can be used to clean greasy pots and pans, regular dishes and cloudy glasses in water below 80 degrees with very little dish soap. This asset can be useful for people with eczema or sensitive skin.

Tawashi can be used to clean almost anything! That includes windows and wheels, people and pets, fixtures and furniture!

You can easily wash the dirt and grime out of tawashi in the washing machine or in the dishwasher.

After washing your tawashi, put it in the sunlight to dry. To keep it smelling fresh, be sure to dry it thoroughly.

Here are a few other tawashi tips:

Don't iron acrylic tawashi.

Don't use or clean acrylic tawashi with chlorine bleach.

Keep acrylic tawashi away from fire. Don't use on or near hot pots, pans or stoves. ∎

Chain

SKILL LEVEL

EASY

FINISHED SIZE
9 inches long

MATERIALS
- Red Heart Super Saver medium (worsted) weight yarn (7 oz/ 364 yds/198g per skein):
  ½ oz/25 yds/14g each #672 spring green, #512 turqua, #994 banana berry and #324 bright yellow
- Size H/8/5mm crochet hook
- Tapestry needle

4 MEDIUM

GAUGE
Gauge is not important for this item.

INSTRUCTIONS
CHAIN
LINK
MAKE 2 WITH BANANA BERRY & 1 EACH WITH SPRING GREEN, BRIGHT YELLOW AND TURQUA.

Row 1: Ch 35, dc in 3rd ch from hook and in each ch across, turn.

Row 2: Ch 2 (*ch-2 does not count as first dc*), dc in first st and in each st across. Leaving 12-inch end, fasten off.

FINISHING
Fold each Link in half and sew short ends tog, forming circle.

Take 1 banana berry Link and fold in half again, tack tog, forming smaller circle for end. Leave rem banana berry Link for other end.

Fold another Link in half and insert end through end Link.

Fold another Link in half and insert 1 end through both ends of last Link. Rep with next Link.

Insert last banana berry through both ends of last Link. Sew ends tog, forming last small circle end. ∎

Fish **Mitt**

SKILL LEVEL

◧■◻◻
EASY

FINISHED SIZE
6 inches wide x 6 inches high

MATERIALS
- Red Heart Super Saver medium (worsted) weight yarn (7 oz/364 yds/198g per skein):
    1 oz/50 yds/28g each #672 spring green and #512 turqua
- Pisgah Yarn & Dyeing Co. Peaches & Crème medium (worsted) weight cotton yarn (2½ oz/122 yds/71g per ball):
    1 ball each #51 apple green and #19 peacock
- Size H/8/5mm crochet hook
- Tapestry needle

GAUGE
Gauge is not important for this item.

PATTERN NOTES
Join with slip stitch as indicated unless otherwise stated.

Chain-3 at beginning of row or round counts as first double crochet unless otherwise stated.

SPECIAL STITCH
Foundation single crochet (foundation sc): Ch 2, insert hook in 2nd ch from hook, yo, pull lp through, yo, pull through 1 lp on hook (*ch-1 completed*), yo, pull through all lps on hook (*sc completed*), [insert hook in ch-1 just completed, yo, pull lp through, yo, pull through 1 lp on hook (*ch-1*), yo, pull through all lps on hook (*sc*)] as indicated.

INSTRUCTIONS
FISH
SIDE
MAKE 1 USING COTTON YARN & 1 USING ACRYLIC YARN.

Row 1: Using spring green or apple green, work 15 **foundation sc** (*see Special Stitch*), turn. (*15 sc*)

Row 2: Ch 1, sc in each st across, **changing colors** (*see Stitch Guide*) to turqua or peacock in last st made, turn.

Row 3: Ch 1, sc in each st across, turn.

Row 4: Ch 1, sc in each st across, changing to spring green or apple green in last st, turn.

Row 5: Ch 1, sc in each st across, turn.

Row 6: Ch 1, sc in each st across, changing to turqua or peacock, turn. Fasten off spring green or apple green.

Row 7: Ch 1, **sc dec** (*see Stitch Guide*) in first 2 sts, sc in each st across, ending with sc dec in last 2 sts, turn. (*13 sc*)

Row 8: Ch 1, sc in each st across, turn.

Row 9: Ch 1, sc dec in first 2 sts, sc in each st across, ending with sc dec in last 2 sts, turn. (*11 sc*)

Row 10: Ch 1, sc in each st across, turn.

Rows 11–14: Ch 1, sc dec in first 2 sts, sc in each st across, ending with sc dec in last 2 sts, turn. At end of last row, fasten off. (*3 sc at end of last row*)

FINISHING
Using **cross-stitch** (*see Fig. 1*), with spring green for acrylic and apple green for cotton Sides, embroider eye on each Side as shown in photo.

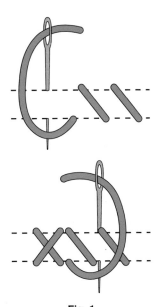

Fig. 1
Cross-Stitch

COTTON SIDE TRIM

On cotton yarn Side, working in starting foundation ch on opposite side of row 1, **join** (*see Pattern Notes*) peacock in first ch, ch 3, 4 dc in same ch, sk next ch, sc in next ch, [sk next ch, 5 dc in next ch, sk next ch, sc in next ch] across. Fasten off.

ASSEMBLY

Join turqua in first ch on opposite side of row 1 on Acrylic side, ch 3, 4 dc in same ch, sk next ch, sc in next ch, [sk next ch, 5 dc in next ch, sk next ch, sc in next ch] across, holding Side pieces WS tog, working through both thicknesses in ends of rows and in sts, evenly sp sc around to opposite edge, join in joining sl st. Fasten off. ■

Double-Stuffed Cookie

SKILL LEVEL

EASY

FINISHED SIZE

3¾ inches in diameter

MATERIALS

- Red Heart Super Saver medium (worsted) weight yarn (7 oz/ 364 yds/198g per skein):
  1 skein each #312 black and #311 white
- Size H/8/5mm crochet hook
- Tapestry needle

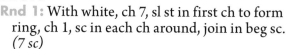

GAUGE

Gauge is not important for this item.

PATTERN NOTES

Join with slip stitch as indicated unless otherwise stated.

Chain-3 at beginning of row or round counts as first double crochet unless otherwise stated.

INSTRUCTIONS

COOKIE
SIDE
MAKE 2.

Rnd 1: With black, make **slip ring** (see Fig. 1), **ch 3** (see Pattern Notes), 11 dc in ring, **join** (see Pattern Notes) in 3rd ch of beg ch-3. Pull to close ring. (12 dc)

Rnd 2: Ch 3, dc in same st, 2 dc in each st around, join in 3rd ch of beg ch-3. (24 dc)

Rnd 3: Ch 3, 2 dc in next st, [dc in next st, 2 dc in next st] around, join in 3rd ch of beg ch-3. Leaving 24-inch end, fasten off. (36 dc)

STUFF

Rnd 1: With white, ch 7, sl st in first ch to form ring, ch 1, sc in each ch around, join in beg sc. (7 sc)

Rnd 2: Ch 1, sc in each st around, join in beg sc.

Next rnds: Rep rnd 2 until piece measures 28 inches from beg. At end of last rnd, leaving 30-inch end, fasten off.

FINISHING

Flatten Stuff; with rnd 1 at center, roll Stuff tog. Tack bottom tog through all layers to hold tog.

Sew 1 Side to top and rem Side to bottom of Stuff. ■

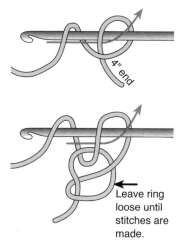

Fig. 1
Slip Ring

Flip-Flop

SKILL LEVEL

EASY

FINISHED SIZE

5¼ x 2½ inches

MATERIALS

- Red Heart Super Saver medium (worsted) weight yarn (7 oz/ 364 yds/198g per skein):
  1 oz/50 yds/28g each #358 lavender
  ½ oz/25 yds/14g #311 white
- Size H/8/5mm crochet hook
- Tapestry needle
- Stitch marker

GAUGE

Gauge is not important for this item.

PATTERN NOTES

Work in continuous rounds, do not turn or join unless otherwise stated.

Mark first stitch of each round.

SPECIAL STITCH

Foundation single crochet (foundation sc): Ch 2, insert hook in 2nd ch from hook, yo, pull lp through, yo, pull through 1 lp on hook *(ch-1 completed)*, yo, pull through all lps on hook *(sc completed)*, [insert hook in ch-1 just completed, yo, pull lp through, yo, pull through 1 lp on hook *(ch-1)*, yo, pull through all lps on hook *(sc)*] as indicated.

INSTRUCTIONS
FLIP-FLOP
SOLE

Rnd 1: With lavender, ch 6, sl st in first ch to form ring, ch 1, sc in each ch around, **do not join rnds** *(see Pattern Notes)*. *(6 sc)*

Rnd 2: Sc in each st around.

Next rnds: Rep rnd 2 until piece measures 29 inches from beg. At end of last rnd, leaving long end, fasten off.

STRAP

Leaving long end at beg, with white, work **foundation sc** *(see Special Stitch)* until piece measures 6 inches from beg. At end of last st, leaving long end, fasten off.

FINISHING

Beg with rnd 1 of Sole, fold up 4 inches, wrap the rem of Sole around the first 4 inches. Sew on bottom to hold in place.

The last part should wrap only about half way down the side to provide a shoe shape.

With long end, tack 1 end of Strap to each side of Sole as shown in photo.

Pull center of Strap to 2nd to last wrap at toe of Sole and tack in place.■

Wicked Witch
Hand

SKILL LEVEL

EASY

FINISHED SIZE

7 inches wide x 6½ inches tall

MATERIALS

- Red Heart Super Saver medium (worsted) weight yarn (7 oz/ 364 yds/198g per skein):
  2 oz/100 yds/57g # 672 spring green
  ½ oz/25 yds/14g #312 black
- Size H/8/5mm crochet hook
- Tapestry needle

GAUGE

Gauge is not important for this item.

PATTERN NOTES

This is for the right hand. If you wish to make a left hand also, work same as right hand except turn it over before working the Finishing.

Join with slip stitch as indicated unless otherwise stated.

INSTRUCTIONS
HAND
PALM

Row 1: With spring green, ch 8, working in **back bar of ch** (*see Fig. 1*), sc in 2nd ch from hook and in back bar of each ch across with 2 sc in last ch, turn. (*8 sc*)

Fig. 1
Back Bar of Chain

Rows 2 & 3: Ch 1, sc in each st across with 2 sc in last st, turn. (*10 sc at end of last row*)

Row 4: Ch 1, 2 sc in first st, sc in each st across with 2 sc in last st, turn. (*12 sc*)

Rows 5–8: Ch 1, sc in each st across, turn.

Row 9: Ch 1, 2 sc in first st, sc in each of next 2 sts, [2 sc in next st, sc in next st] across, turn. (*16 sc*)

Row 10: Ch 1, sc in each st across, turn.

Row 11: Ch 1, sc in each of first 11 sts, sl st in next st, leaving rem sts unworked, turn. (*11 sc*)

Row 12: Ch 1, sk sl st, sc in each st across, turn.

Row 13: Ch 1, sc in each st across, turn.

FINGERS
INDEX
Row 1: Ch 1, sc in each of first 3 sts, leaving rem sts unworked, turn.

Rows 2–5: Ch 1, sc in each st across, turn.

Row 6: Ch 1, **sc dec** (*see Stitch Guide*) in first 2 sts, sc in last st, turn.

Row 7: Ch 1, sc dec in 2 sts. Fasten off.

PINKY
Row 1: Join spring green with sc in first st at right edge of Palm, sc in next st, leaving rem sts unworked, turn. (*2 sc*)

Rows 2 & 3: Ch 1, sc in each st across, turn.

Row 4: Ch 1, sc dec in 2 sts. Fasten off.

RING
Row 1: Join spring green with sc in next unworked st on Palm from Pinky, sc in each of next 2 sts, leaving rem sts unworked, turn.
(*3 sc*)

Rows 2–4: Ch 1, sc in each st across, turn.

Row 5: Ch 1, sc dec in first 2 sts, sc in last st, turn.

Row 6: Ch 1, sc dec in 2 sts. Fasten off.

MIDDLE
Row 1: Join spring green with sc in next unworked st on Palm from Ring, sc in each of last 2 unworked sts, turn. (*3 sc*)

Rows 2–6: Ch 1, sc in each st across, turn.

Row 7: Ch 1, sc dec in first 2 sts, sc in last st, turn.

Row 8: Ch 1, sc dec in 2 sts. Fasten off.

THUMB
Row 1: Sk next unworked st on row 11 of Palm next to Index Finger, join spring green with sc in next st, sc in each of next 3 sts, turn. (*4 sc*)

Rows 2 & 3: Ch 1, sc in each st across, turn.

Row 4: Ch 1, sc dec in first 2 sts, sc dec in last 2 sts, turn. (*2 sc*)

Row 5: Ch 1, sc dec in 2 sts. Fasten off.

FINISHING
Working around outer edge, in ends of rows and in **back lps** (*see Stitch Guide*) of sts and chs, **join** (*see Pattern Notes*) black in end of row 1, evenly sp sl st around, join in beg sl st. Fasten off. ∎

Spiral

SKILL LEVEL

EASY

FINISHED SIZE
4 inches in diameter

MATERIALS
- Caron Simply Brites medium (worsted) weight yarn (6 oz/ 315 yds/85g per skein): 1 oz/50 yds/28g each #9607 limelight, #9610 grape and #9604 watermelon

4 MEDIUM

- Size H/8/5mm crochet hook
- Tapestry needle

GAUGE
Gauge is not important for this item.

SPECIAL STITCH
Foundation single crochet (foundation sc): Ch 2, insert hook in 2nd ch from hook, yo, pull lp through, yo, pull through 1 lp on hook (*ch-1 completed*), yo, pull through all lps on hook (*sc completed*), [insert hook in ch-1 just completed, yo, pull lp through, yo, pull through 1 lp on hook (*ch-1*), yo, pull through all lps on hook (*sc*)] as indicated.

INSTRUCTIONS
SPIRAL
Row 1: With limelight, work 20 **foundation sc** (*see Special Stitch*), turn. (*20 sc*)

Rows 2 & 3: Ch 1, 2 sc in first st, sc in each st across with **sc dec** (*see Stitch Guide*) in last 2 sts, turn.

Row 4: Ch 1, 2 sc in first st, sc in each st across with sc dec in last 2 sts, **changing colors** (*see Stitch Guide*) to watermelon in last st, turn.

Rows 5–7: Ch 1, 2 sc in first st, sc in each st across with sc dec in last 2 sts, turn.

Row 8: Ch 1, 2 sc in first st, sc in each st across with sc dec in last 2 sts, changing to grape in last st, turn.

Rows 9–12: Rep rows 5–8, changing to limelight.

Rows 13–16: Rep rows 5–8, changing to watermelon.

Rows 17–20: Rep rows 5–8.

Rows 21–23: Rep rows 5–7.

Last row: 2 sc in first st, sc in each st across with sc dec in last 2 sts. Fasten off.

FINISHING
Sew first and Last rows tog.

Run piece of yarn through ends of rows, pull to close, secure end.

Rep on rem end. ■

Puzzle

FINISHED SIZE
4 inches square

MATERIALS
- Red Heart Super Saver medium (worsted) weight yarn (7 oz/ 364 yds/198g per skein):
  1 oz/ 50 yds/28g each #672 spring green, #512 turqua, # 718 shocking pink and #324 bright yellow
- Size H/8/5mm crochet hook
- Tapestry needle

4 MEDIUM

GAUGE
Gauge is not important for this item.

INSTRUCTIONS
PUZZLE
STRIP
MAKE 1 OF EACH COLOR.
Row 1: Ch 25, sc in **back bar** (*see Fig. 1*) of 2nd ch from hook and in back bar of each ch across, turn. (*24 sc*)

Rows 2–5: Working in **back lps** (*see Stitch Guide*), ch 1, sc in each st across, turn. At end of last row, fasten off.

Row 6: Working in starting ch on opposite side of row 1, join with sc in first ch, sc in each ch across. Fasten off.

FINISHING
Folding Strips in half according to Assembly Diagram (*see Fig 2*), sew short ends of each Strip tog. ■

Fig. 1
Back Bar of Chain

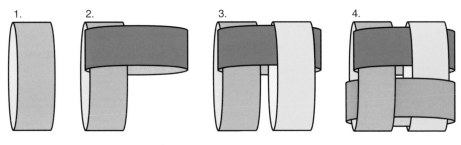

1. 2. 3. 4.

Fig. 2
Puzzle
Assembly Diagram

Sunrise Mitt

SKILL LEVEL

EASY

FINISHED SIZE

6½ x 7½ inches

MATERIALS

- Red Heart Super Saver medium (worsted) weight yarn (7 oz/ 364 yds/198g per skein):
  1 skein #319 cherry red
  1 oz/50 yds/28g each #254 pumpkin and #324 bright yellow
- Size H/8/5mm crochet hook
- Tapestry needle

4
MEDIUM

GAUGE

Gauge is not important for this item.

SPECIAL STITCHES

Foundation single crochet (foundation sc): Ch 2, insert hook in 2nd ch from hook, yo, pull lp through, yo, pull through 1 lp on hook (*ch-1 completed*), yo, pull through all lps on hook (*sc completed*), [insert hook in ch-1 just completed, yo, pull lp through, yo, pull through 1 lp on hook (*ch-1*), yo, pull through all lps on hook (*sc*)] as indicated.

Loop stitch (lp st): With WS facing, pull up long lp (*see 1 of Fig. 1*), insert hook

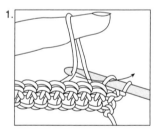

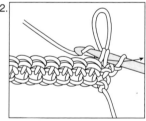

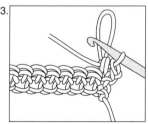

Fig. 1
Loop Stitch

in st, pull lp through, yo, pull lp through all lps on hook (*see 2 and 3 of Fig. 1*). Loop will be on RS of work.

INSTRUCTIONS
MITT
FRONT

Row 1: With cherry red, work 30 **foundation sc** (*see Special Stitches*), turn.

Rows 2–5: Ch 1, sc in each st across, turn.

Row 6: Ch 1, sc in first st, **lp st** (*see Special Stitches*) in each of next 18 sts, sc in last st, turn.

Row 7: Ch 1, sc in each st across, turn.

Row 8: Ch 1, sc in first st, lp st in each of next 18 sts, sc in last st, turn.

Row 9: Ch 1, sc in each st across, turn.

Row 10: Ch 1, sc in first st, lp st in each of next 18 sts, sc in last st, turn.

Row 11: Ch 1, sc in each st across, **changing colors** (*see Stitch Guide*) to pumpkin in last st, turn. Leaving long end, fasten off cherry red.

Row 12: Ch 1, sc in first st, lp st in each of next 18 sts, sc in last st, turn.

Row 13: Ch 1, **sc dec** (*see Stitch Guide*) in first 2 sts, sc in each st across with sc dec in last 2 sts, turn. (*18 sc*)

Row 14: Ch 1, sc in first st, lp st in each of next 16 sts, sc in last st, turn.

Row 15: Ch 1, sc dec in first 2 sts, sc in each st across with sc dec in last 2 sts, turn. (*16 sc*)

Row 16: Ch 1, sc in first st, lp st in each of next 14 sts, sc in last st, turn.

Row 17: Ch 1, sc dec in first 2 sts, sc in each st across with sc dec in last 2 sts, changing to bright yellow in last st, turn. Leaving long end, fasten off pumpkin. *(14 sc)*

Row 18: Ch 1, sc in first st, sc dec in next 2 sts, lp st in each of next 8 sts, sc dec in next 2 sts, sc in last st, turn. *(12 sts)*

Row 19: Ch 1, sc dec in first 2 sts, sc in each st across with sc dec in last 2 sts, turn. *(10 sc)*

Row 20: Ch 1, sc dec in first 2 sts, sc in each st across with sc dec in last 2 sts. Leaving long end, fasten off. *(8 sc)*

BACK
Row 1: With cherry red, work 30 foundation sc, turn.

Rows 2–10: Ch 1, sc in each st across, turn.

Row 11: Ch 1, sc in each st across, changing to pumpkin in last st, turn. Leaving long end, fasten off cherry red.

Row 12: Ch 1, sc in each st across, turn.

Row 13: Ch 1, sc dec in first 2 sts, sc in each st across with sc dec in last 2 sts, turn. *(18 sc)*

Row 14: Ch 1, sc in each st across, turn.

Row 15: Ch 1, sc dec in first 2 sts, sc in each st across with sc dec in last 2 sts, turn. *(16 sc)*

Row 16: Ch 1, sc in each st across, turn.

Row 17: Ch 1, sc dec in first 2 sts, sc in each st across with sc dec in last 2 sts, changing to bright yellow in last st, turn. Leaving long end, fasten off pumpkin. *(14 sc)*

Row 18: Ch 1, sc in first st, sc dec in next 2 sts, sc in each st across to last 3 sts, sc dec in next 2 sts, sc in last st, turn. *(12 sc)*

Row 19: Ch 1, sc dec in first 2 sts, sc in each st across with sc dec in last 2 sts, turn. *(10 sc)*

Row 20: Ch 1, sc dec in first 2 sts, sc in each st across with sc dec in last 2 sts. Leaving long end, fasten off. *(8 sc)*

FINISHING
Holding Front and Back WS tog, working in ends of rows and using matching long ends, join cherry red with sc in end of row 1, matching colors, evenly sp sc across to opposite side of row 1. Fasten off. ∎

Rose

SKILL LEVEL

EASY

FINISHED SIZE
5 inches across, including Leaves

MATERIALS
- Red Heart Super Saver medium (worsted) weight yarn (7 oz/364 yds/198g per skein):
  2 oz/100 yds/57g #718 shocking pink
  ½ oz/25 yds/14g #672 spring green
- Size H/8/5mm crochet hook
- Tapestry needle
- Stitch marker

GAUGE
Gauge is not important for this item.

PATTERN NOTES
Work in continuous rounds, do not turn or join unless otherwise stated.

Mark first stitch of each round.

INSTRUCTIONS
ROSE
Rnd 1: With shocking pink, ch 7, sl st in first ch to form ring, ch 1, sc in each ch around, **do not join** (*see Pattern Notes*). (*7 sc*)

Rnd 2: Sc in each st around.

Next rnds: Rep rnd 2 until piece measures 24 inches from beg. At end of last rnd, leaving long end, fasten off.

LEAF
MAKE 2.
Rnd 1: With spring green, make **slip ring** (*see Fig. 1*), ch 1, 4 sc in ring, **do not join**. Pull ring closed. (*4 sc*)

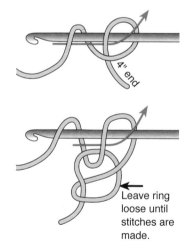

Leave ring loose until stitches are made.

Fig. 1
Slip Ring

Rnd 2: [Sc in first st, 2 sc in next st] around. (*6 sc*)

Next rnds: Rep rnd 2 until piece measures 1 inch from beg.

Next rnd: Ch 1, sc in each st around.

Next rnds: Rep last rnd until piece measures 2 inches from beg. At end of last rnd, leaving long end, fasten off.

FINISHING
Beg with rnd of Rose in center, flatten and roll tightly tog.

Sew tog on bottom as you roll to hold tog.

Slightly gather and sew last rnd of each Leaf to top of Rose as shown in photo. ■

Red Apple

SKILL LEVEL

EASY

FINISHED SIZE
5¼ x 7½ inches, including stem

MATERIALS
- Caron Simply Soft medium (worsted) weight yarn (6 oz/ 315 yds/170g per skein):
  3 oz/150 yds/85g #9729 red
  ½ oz/25 yds/14g #9727 black
- Caron Simply Brites medium (worsted) weight yarn (6 oz/315 yds/ 85g per skein):
  ½ oz/25 yds/14g #9607 limelight
- Size H/8/5mm crochet hook
- Tapestry needle
- Stitch marker

GAUGE
Gauge is not important for this item.

PATTERN NOTES
Join with slip stitch as indicated unless otherwise stated.

Work in continuous rounds, do not turn or join unless otherwise stated.

Mark first stitch of round.

INSTRUCTIONS
APPLE
SIDE
MAKE 2.
Row 1 (RS): Beg at bottom edge, with red, ch 7, sc in 2nd ch from hook and in each ch across, turn. *(6 sc)*

Rows 2–7: Ch 1, 2 sc in first st, sc in each st across with 2 sc in last st, turn. *(18 sc at end of last row)*

Rows 8–19: Ch 1, sc in each st across, turn.

Rows 20–23: Ch 1, **sc dec** *(see Stitch Guide)* in first 2 sts, sc in each st across with sc dec in last 2 sts, turn. At end of last row, fasten off. *(10 sc at end of last row)*

ASSEMBLY

Holding WS of Sides tog, working in ends of rows and through both thicknesses, **join** *(see Pattern Notes)* red in end of 3rd row from top edge, evenly sp sl st around to opposite end of 3rd row. Leaving top edge open, fasten off.

STEM

Rnd 1: With black, ch 6, sl st in first ch to form ring, ch 1, sc in each ch around, **do not join** *(see Pattern Notes)*.

Rnd 2: Sc in each st around.

Next rnds: Rep rnd 2 until piece measures 2½ inches from beg. Leaving long end, fasten off.

With long end, sew Stem to top edge on 1 Side piece for front.

LEAF

Row 1: With limelight, ch 6, sc in 2nd ch from hook and in each ch across, turn. *(5 sc)*

Rows 2–4: Ch 1, sc dec in first 2 sts, sc in each st across, turn. *(2 sc at end of last row)*

Row 5: Ch 1, sc dec in 2 sts. Leaving long end, fasten off.

With long end, sew Leaf to front Side as shown in photo. ∎

Octopus

SKILL LEVEL

EASY

FINISHED SIZE

9 inches long

MATERIALS

- Caron Simply Brites medium (worsted) weight yarn (6 oz/ 315 yds/85g per skein):
  1 skein #9604 watermelon
  ¼ oz/12 yds/7g #9607 limelight
- Size H/8/5mm crochet hook
- Tapestry needle
- Stitch marker

GAUGE

Gauge is not important for this item.

PATTERN NOTES

Work in continuous rounds, do not turn or join unless otherwise stated.

Mark first stitch of each round.

INSTRUCTIONS
OCTOPUS
BODY

Rnd 1: With watermelon, ch 2, 6 sc in 2nd ch from hook, **do not join** *(see Pattern Notes)*. *(6 sc)*

Rnd 2: 2 sc in each st around. *(12 sc)*

Rnd 3: [Sc in next st, 2 sc in next st] around. *(18 sc)*

Rnd 4: [Sc in each of next 2 sts, 2 sc in next st] around. *(24 sc)*

Rnds 5–12: Sc in each st around.

ARMS
Ch 1, [sc in next st, ch 20, 2 dc in 3rd ch from hook, 3 dc in each ch across, sc in each of next 2 sts on rnd 12] around, join with sl st in beg sc. Fasten off.

FINISHING
Using **cross-stitch** *(see Fig. 1)*, with 2 strands of limelight, embroider eyes as shown in photo. ■

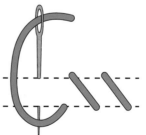

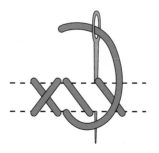

Fig. 1
Cross-Stitch

Black Cat

SKILL LEVEL

EASY

FINISHED SIZE
6 x 5 inches, including Ears

MATERIALS
- Red Heart Super Saver medium (worsted) weight yarn (7 oz/ 364 yds/198g per skein):
  1 skein #312 black
  ½ oz/25 yds/14g each #672 spring green, #311 white and #373 petal pink
- Size H/8/5mm crochet hook
- Tapestry needle
- Stitch marker

GAUGE
Gauge is not important for this item.

PATTERN NOTES
Work in continuous rounds, do not turn or join unless otherwise stated.

Mark first stitch of round.

INSTRUCTIONS
CAT
FACE
Rnd 1: With black, ch 7, sl st in first ch to form ring, ch 1, sc in each ch around, **do not join** *(see Pattern Notes)*. *(7 sc)*

Rnd 2: Sc in each st around.

Next rnds: Rep rnd 2 until piece measures 24 inches long. At end of last rnd, leaving 30-inch end, fasten off.

EAR
MAKE 2.
Row 1: With black, leaving 10-inch end at beg, ch 7, sc in 2nd ch from hook and in each ch across, turn. *(6 sc)*

Row 2: Ch 1, **sc dec** *(see Stitch Guide)* in first 2 sts, sc in each st across, turn. *(5 sc)*

Rows 3–5: Rep row 2. *(2 sc at end of last row)*

Row 6: Ch 1, sc dec in next 2 sts. Fasten off.

ASSEMBLY
Flatten Face tube and roll tightly tog with rnd 1 at center of roll, tack tog on bottom through all layers so that all layers stay connected.

Sew Ears to top of Face as shown in photo.

FINISHING

Using **lazy daisy stitch** (*see Fig. 1*), with spring green, embroider eyes on Face as shown in photo.

Using **satin stitch** (*see Fig. 2*), with petal pink, embroider nose centered below eyes as shown in photo.

Using **straight stitch** (*see Fig. 3*), with white, embroider 3 whiskers on each side of nose as shown in photo. ■

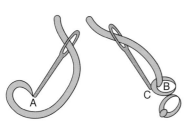

Fig. 1
Lazy Daisy Stitch

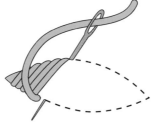

Fig. 2
Satin Stitch

Fig. 3
Straight Stitch

Butterfly

SKILL LEVEL

EASY

FINISHED SIZE

7 inches square, excluding antennae

MATERIALS

- Red Heart Super Saver medium (worsted) weight yarn (7 oz/ 364 yds/198g per skein):
    1 skein #319 cherry red
    ½ oz/25 yds/14g each #358 lavender,
    #718 shocking pink and #312 black
- Size H/8/5mm crochet hook
- Tapestry needle

GAUGE

Gauge is not important for this item.

PATTERN NOTES

Join with slip stitch as indicated unless otherwise stated.

Chain-3 at beginning of row or round counts as first double crochet unless otherwise stated.

INSTRUCTIONS
BUTTERFLY
WING
MAKE 2.

Rnd 1: With lavender, make **slip ring** (see Fig. 1), ch 5 (counts as first dc and ch-2), [dc in ring, ch 2] 6 times, dc in ring, join with hdc in 3rd ch of beg ch-5, forming last ch sp, pull to close ring. Fasten off.

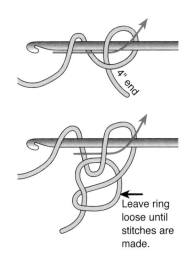

Leave ring loose until stitches are made.

Fig. 1
Slip Ring

Rnd 2: Join (see Pattern Notes) shocking pink in last ch sp formed, **ch 3** (see Pattern Notes), (dc, ch 2, 2 dc) in same ch sp, sc in next ch sp, [(2 dc, ch 2, 2 dc) in next ch sp, sc in next ch sp] around, join in 3rd ch of beg ch-3.

Rnd 3: Sl st in next st and in next ch sp, ch 3, (2 dc, ch 2, 3 dc) in same ch sp, *ch 1, sc in next sc, ch 1**, (3 dc, ch 2, 3 dc) in next ch sp, rep from * around, ending last rep at **, join in 3rd ch of beg ch-3. Fasten off.

Rnd 4: Join lavender in first st, ch 4 (counts as first dc and ch-1 sp), *sk next st, dc in next st, ch 1, (dc, ch 1) 3 times in next ch sp, dc in next st, ch 1, sk next st, dc in next st, ch 2, sc in next sc, ch 2**, dc in next st, ch 1, rep from * around, ending last rep at **, join in 3rd ch of beg ch-4. Fasten off.

Rnd 5: Join cherry red in first st, ch 3, *2 dc in next ch-1 sp, dc in next dc, 2 dc in next dc, dc in next ch-1 sp, 3 dc in next dc, dc in next ch-1 sp, 2 dc in next dc, dc in next dc, 2 dc in next ch-1 sp, dc in next dc, ch 1, sc in next sc, ch 1**, dc in next dc, rep from * around, ending last rep at **, join in 3rd ch of beg ch-3.

Rnd 6: Sl st in next st, ch 1, sc in same st, ch 1, *[dc in next dc, ch-1] 13 times, sc in next dc, sk next dc, next ch-1 sp, next sc, next ch-1 sp and next dc**, sc in next dc, ch 1, rep from * around, ending last rep at **, join in beg sc. Fasten off.

BODY

With black, ch 2, yo, insert hook in 2nd ch from hook, yo, pull lp through, yo, pull lp through 1 lp on hook (ch-1 completed), yo, pull through all lps on hook (hdc completed), *yo, insert hook in last ch completed, yo, pull lp through, yo, pull through 1 lp on hook (ch-1), yo, pull through all lps on hook (hdc), rep from * for 20 inches. At end of last st, fasten off.

FINISHING

Holding Wings WS tog, wrap Body around center of both Wings as shown in photo. Tie Body ends in knot for head, leaving ends for antennae.

Sew Body to Wings. ∎

Flower Mitt

SKILL LEVEL

EASY

FINISHED SIZE

5½ x 5¾ inches

MATERIALS

- Caron Simply Brites medium (worsted) weight yarn (6 oz/ 315 yds/ 85g per skein):
  1 oz/25 yds/14g each #9607 limelight, #9609 berry blue and #9608 blue mint
- Size H/8/5mm crochet hook
- Tapestry needle

GAUGE

Gauge is not important for this item.

INSTRUCTIONS

MITT
SIDE
MAKE 2.

Row 1: With berry blue, ch 21, sc in **back bar** *(see Fig. 1)* of 2nd ch from hook and in back bar of each ch across, turn. *(20 sc)*

Fig. 1
Back Bar of Chain

Rows 2–5: Ch 1 sc in each st across, turn.

Row 6: Ch 1, sc in each st across, **changing colors** *(see Stitch Guide)* to blue mint in last st, turn. Fasten off berry blue.

Rows 7–11: Ch 1, sc in each st across, turn.

Row 12: Ch 1, sc in each st across, changing to limelight in last st, turn. Fasten off blue mint.

Rows 13–17: Ch 1, sc in each st across, turn.

Row 18: Ch 1, sc in each st across, changing to berry blue in last st, turn. Fasten off limelight.

Rows 19 & 20: Ch 1, sc in each st across, turn.

Rows 21–23: Ch 1, **sc dec** *(see Stitch Guide)* in first 2 sts, sc in each st across with sc dec in last 2 sts, turn. *(14 sc at end of last row)*

Row 24: Ch 1, sc dec in first 2 sts, sc in each st across with sc dec in last 2 sts. Fasten off. *(12 sc)*

FINISHING

Holding Side pieces tog, working in ends of rows and in sts through both thicknesses, join blue mint with sl st in end of row 1, evenly sp sl st around to opposite end of row 1. Fasten off.

FLOWER

With blue mint, ch 4, sl st in first ch to form ring, (sl st, ch 3, tr, ch 3) 6 times in ring, join with sl st in beg sl st. Leaving long end, fasten off.

Sew to Mitt as shown in photo. ■

Orange Face

SKILL LEVEL

EASY

FINISHED SIZE

7 inches in diameter

MATERIALS

- Red Heart Super Saver medium (worsted) weight yarn (7 oz/ 364 yds/198g per skein):
  1 skein #254 pumpkin
  ½ oz/25 yds/14g each #324 bright yellow, #718 shocking pink, #347 light periwinkle and #312 black

4 MEDIUM

- Size H/8/5mm crochet hook
- Tapestry needle

GAUGE

Gauge is not important for this item.

PATTERN NOTES

Join with slip stitch as indicated unless otherwise stated.

Chain-3 at beginning of round counts as first double crochet unless otherwise stated.

SPECIAL STITCHES

Surface stitch (surface st): Holding yarn at back of work, insert hook in sp between sts, yo, pull lp through sp and lp on hook.

Loop stitch (lp st): With WS facing, pull up long lp (*see 1 of Fig. 1*), insert hook in st, pull lp through, yo, pull lp through all lps on hook (*see 2 and 3 of Fig. 1*). Loop will be on RS of work.

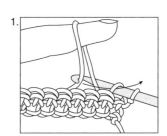

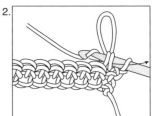

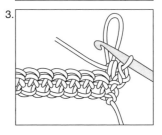

Fig. 1
Loop Stitch

INSTRUCTIONS
ORANGE FACE
CIRCLE
MAKE 2.

Rnd 1: With pumpkin, make **slip ring** *(see Fig. 2)*, **ch 3** *(see Pattern Notes)*, 11 dc in ring, **join** *(see Pattern Notes)* in 3rd ch of beg ch-3. Pull to close ring. *(12 dc)*

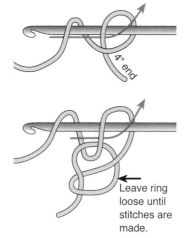

Fig. 2
Slip Ring

Rnd 2: Ch 3, dc in same st, 2 dc in each st around, join in 3rd ch of beg ch-3. *(24 dc)*

Rnd 3: Ch 3, 2 dc in next st, [dc in next st, 2 dc in next st] around, join in 3rd ch of beg ch-3. *(36 dc)*

Rnd 4: Ch 3, dc in next st, 2 dc in next st, [dc in each of next 2 sts, 2 dc in next st] around, join in 3rd ch of beg ch-3. *(48 dc)*

Rnd 5: Ch 3, dc in each of next 2 sts, 2 dc in next st, [dc in each of next 3 sts, 2 dc in next st] around, join in 3rd ch of beg ch-3. Fasten off. *(60 dc)*

EYE
MAKE 2.

Rnd 1: With black, make slip ring, ch 1, 6 sc in ring, join in beg sc. Pull to close ring. Fasten off. *(6 sc)*

Rnd 2: Join light periwinkle with sc in first st, sc in same st, 2 sc in each st around, join in beg sc. Leaving long end, fasten off.

Sew Eyes over rnds 3 and 4 on 1 Circle ¾ inch apart for face.

Using **surface st** *(see Special Stitches)*, with hot pink, work smile centered below eyes as shown in photo.

Using **lp st** *(see Special Stitches)*, working in **back lps** *(see Stitch Guide)* of face, with yellow, work hair across top edge as shown in photo.

Rep on rem Circle.

Holding Circles WS tog, leaving 4 inches at bottom edges open, with pumpkin, sc circles tog, working in rem lps at top across hair. Fasten off.

Work 2 rows of lp st across top edge in sts just worked. ■

Puzzle Ball

SKILL LEVEL

EASY

FINISHED SIZE
4 inches in diameter

MATERIALS
- Pisgah Yarn & Dyeing Co. Peaches & Crème medium (worsted) weight cotton yarn (2½ oz/122 yds/ 71g per ball):
    1 ball each #51 apple green and #31 shocking pink
- Size H/8/5mm crochet hook
- Tapestry needle

4 MEDIUM

GAUGE
Gauge is not important for this item.

SPECIAL STITCH
Foundation half double crochet (foundation hdc):
    Ch 2, yo, insert hook in 2nd ch from hook, yo, pull lp through, yo, pull through 1 lp on hook *(ch-1 completed)*, yo, pull through all lps on hook *(hdc completed)*, [yo, insert hook in ch-1 just completed, yo, pull lp through, yo, pull through 1 lp on hook *(ch-1)*, yo, pull through all lps on hook *(hdc)*] as indicated.

INSTRUCTIONS
BALL
Row 1: With shocking pink, work **foundation hdc** *(see Special Stitch)* for 20 inches. At end of last st, fasten off.

Row 2: Join apple green with sl st in first st, hdc in same st and in each st across. Fasten off.

Row 3: With shocking pink, rep row 2.

Row 4: Rep row 2.

Row 5: Join shocking pink with sl st in first st, hdc in same st and in each st across. Leaving long end, fasten off.

FINISHING
Fold according to **Folding Diagram** *(see Fig. 1).*

Sew short ends tog. ■

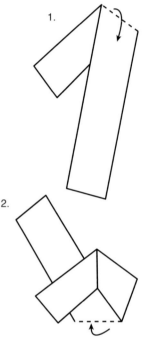
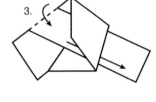
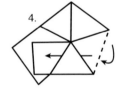

Fig. 1
Puzzle Ball
Folding Diagram

Flower

SKILL LEVEL

EASY

FINISHED SIZE
6½ inches in diameter

MATERIALS
- Red Heart Super Saver medium (worsted) weight yarn (7 oz/ 364 yds/198g per skein):
    2 oz/100 yds/57g each #718 shocking pink and #319 cherry red
    ½ oz/25 yds/14g #324 bright yellow
- Size H/8/5mm crochet hook
- Tapestry needle
- Stitch marker

GAUGE
Gauge is not important for this item.

PATTERN NOTES
Join with slip stitch as indicated unless otherwise stated.

Work in continuous rounds, do not turn or join unless otherwise stated.

Mark first stitch of each round.

Chain-3 at beginning of row or round counts as first double crochet unless otherwise stated.

INSTRUCTIONS
FLOWER
Rnd 1: With bright yellow, ch 4, sl st in first ch to form ring, (sl st, ch 3, tr, ch 3) 6 times in ring, **join** (see Pattern Notes) in beg sl st. Fasten off. (6 petals)

Rnd 2: Working behind petals, join shocking pink in any sl st, ch 4, [sl st in next sl st, ch 4] around, **do not join** (see Pattern Notes).

Rnd 3: [Sl st in next ch sp, (ch 3, tr, ch 3, sl st) 3 times in same ch sp] around. Fasten off.

Rnd 4: Working behind petals, join cherry red in any sl st, ch 4, [sl st in next sl st, ch 4] around, do not join.

Rnd 5: (Sl st, ch 3, tr, ch 3, sl st) twice in next ch sp and in each ch sp around. Fasten off.

BACK
Rnd 1: With shocking pink, make **slip ring** (see Fig. 1), **ch 3** (see Pattern Notes), 11 dc in center of ring, join in 3rd ch of beg ch-3. Pull to close ring. (12 dc)

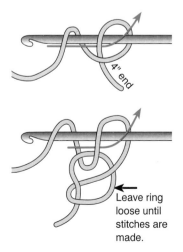

4" end

Leave ring loose until stitches are made.

Fig. 1
Slip Ring

Rnd 2: Ch 3, dc in same st, 2 dc in each st around, join in 3rd ch of beg ch-3. *(24 dc)*

Rnd 3: Ch 3, 2 dc in next st, [dc in next st, 2 dc in next st] around, join in 3rd ch of beg ch-3. Leaving long end, fasten off.

FINISHING
Sew Back to WS of Flower, leaving about 4 inches open for hand. ■

Froggy Mitt

SKILL LEVEL
■■□□
EASY

FINISHED SIZE
8 x 10 inches

MATERIALS
- Red Heart Super Saver medium (worsted) weight yarn (7 oz/ 364 yds/198g per skein):
    2 oz/100 yds/57g # 672 spring green
    ½ oz/25 yds/14g each #311 white and #312 black
- Pisgah Yarn & Dyeing Co. Peaches & Crème medium (worsted) weight cotton yarn (2½ oz/122 yds/71g per ball):
    1 ball #51 apple green
- Size H/8/5mm crochet hook
- Tapestry needle
- Stitch marker

GAUGE
Gauge is not important for this item.

PATTERN NOTE
Join with slip stitch as indicated unless otherwise stated.

SPECIAL STITCHES
Foundation single crochet (foundation sc): Ch 2, insert hook in 2nd ch from hook, yo, pull lp through, yo, pull through 1 lp on hook *(ch-1 completed)*, yo, pull through all lps on hook *(sc completed)*, [insert hook in ch-1 just completed, yo, pull lp through, yo, pull through 1 lp on hook *(ch-1)*, yo, pull through all lps on hook *(sc)*] as indicated.

Surface stitch (surface st): Holding yarn at back of work, insert hook in sp between sts, yo, pull lp through sp and lp on hook.

INSTRUCTIONS
FROG
BODY
MAKE 1 USING COTTON YARN & 1 USING ACRYLIC YARN.
Row 1: Using spring green or apple green, work 17 **foundation sc** *(see Special Stitches)*, turn. *(17 sc)*

Rows 2–7: Ch 1, sc in each st across, turn.

Row 8: Ch 1, 2 sc in first st, sc in each st across with 2 sc in last st, turn. *(19 sc)*

Row 9: Ch 1, sc in each st across, turn.

Row 10: Ch 1, 2 sc in first st, sc in each st across with 2 sc in last st, turn. *(21 sc)*

Row 11: Ch 1, sc in each st across, turn.

Row 12: Ch 1, 2 sc in first st, sc in each st across with 2 sc in last st, turn. *(23 sc)*

Row 13: Ch 1, sc in each st across, turn.

Row 14: Ch 1, 2 sc in first st, sc in each st across with 2 sc in last st, turn. *(25 sc)*

Row 15: Ch 1, sc in each st across, turn.

FIRST LEG

Row 1: Ch 1, sc in each of first 5 sts, leaving rem sts unworked, turn. *(5 sc)*

Rows 2 & 3: Ch 1, sc in each st across, turn.

Row 4: Ch 1, **sc dec** *(see Stitch Guide)* in first 2 sts, sc in next st, sc dec in last 2 sts, turn. *(3 sc)*

Row 5: Ch 1, sc dec in first 2 sts, sc in last st. Fasten off.

2ND LEG

Row 1: Turn piece, beg at other end of row 15 on Frog, join spring green with sc in first st, sc in each of next 4 sts, leaving rem sts unworked, turn. *(5 sc)*

Rows 2 & 3: Ch 1, sc in each st across, turn.

Row 4: Ch 1, sc dec in first 2 sts, sc in next st, sc dec in last 2 sts, turn. *(3 sc)*

Row 5: Ch 1, sc dec in first 2 sts, sc in last st. Fasten off.

HEAD

Row 1: Sk next st on row 15 of Body, join with sc in next st, sc in each of next 12 sts, leaving last st unworked, turn. *(13 sc)*

Rows 2–4: Ch 1, sc in each st across, turn.

Rows 5–8: Ch 1, sc in first st, sc dec in next 2 sts, sc in each st across to last 3 sts, sc dec in next 2 sts, sc in last st, turn. *(5 sc at end of last row)*

Row 9: Ch 1, sc dec in first 2 sts, sc in next st, sc dec in last 2 sts. Fasten off.

EYE
MAKE 2.
Rnd 1: With black, work **slip ring** *(see Fig. 1)*, ch 1, 6 sc in ring, **join** *(see Pattern Note)* in beg sc. Pull to close ring. Fasten off.

Rnd 2: Join white in first st, ch 3 *(counts as first dc)*, dc in same st, 2 dc in each st around, join in 3rd ch of beg ch-3. Leaving long end, fasten off.

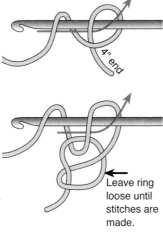

Leave ring loose until stitches are made.

Fig. 1
Slip Ring

FINISHING
Puff the Eyes so they do not lie flat, sew last rnd of Eyes to acrylic Head for face as shown in photo.

Using **surface st** *(see Special Stitches)*, with black, work mouth as shown in photo.

Holding Side pieces tog, with face facing, working in ends of rows, join spring green with sc in end of row 1, evenly sp sc around to opposite end of row 1. Fasten off. ■

Folded Square

SKILL LEVEL

EASY

FINISHED SIZE
6 inches square

MATERIALS
- Caron Simply Soft Brites medium (worsted) weight yarn (6 oz/ 315 yds/ 85g per skein): 1 oz/50 yds/28g each #9607 limelight and #9606 lemonade
- Size H/8/5mm crochet hook
- Tapestry needle
- Stitch marker

GAUGE
Gauge is not important for this item.

INSTRUCTIONS
SQUARE

Row 1: With limelight, ch 16, sc in 2nd ch from hook and in each ch across, turn.

Rows 2–15: Ch 1, sc in each st across, turn.

Row 16: Ch 1, sc in each st across, **changing colors** *(see Stitch Guide)* to lemonade in last st, turn. Leaving long end, fasten off limelight.

Rows 17–32: Ch 1, sc in each st across, turn. At end of last row, change to limelight. Leaving long end, fasten off lemonade.

Next rows: Rep rows 17–32, changing to lemonade. Leaving long end, fasten off limelight.

Next rows: Rep rows 17–32. At end of last row, fasten off.

FINISHING
Folding corners in according to **Folding Diagram** *(see Fig. 1)*, and using long ends, sew edges tog where they touch as you fold. ■

1.

2.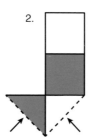

3.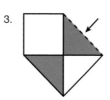

4.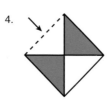

Fig. 1
Folded Square
Folding Diagram

Stitch Guide

For more complete information, visit **FreePatterns.com**

ABBREVIATIONS

beg	begin/begins/beginning
bpdc	back post double crochet
bpsc	back post single crochet
bptr	back post treble crochet
CC	contrasting color
ch(s)	chain(s)
ch-	refers to chain or space previously made (e.g., ch-1 space)
ch sp(s)	chain space(s)
cl(s)	cluster(s)
cm	centimeter(s)
dc	double crochet (singular/plural)
dc dec	double crochet 2 or more stitches together, as indicated
dec	decrease/decreases/decreasing
dtr	double treble crochet
ext	extended
fpdc	front post double crochet
fpsc	front post single crochet
fptr	front post treble crochet
g	gram(s)
hdc	half double crochet
hdc dec	half double crochet 2 or more stitches together, as indicated
inc	increase/increases/increasing
lp(s)	loop(s)
MC	main color
mm	millimeter(s)
oz	ounce(s)
pc	popcorn(s)
rem	remain/remains/remaining
rep(s)	repeat(s)
rnd(s)	round(s)
RS	right side
sc	single crochet (singular/plural)
sc dec	single crochet 2 or more stitches together, as indicated
sk	skip/skipped/skipping
sl st(s)	slip stitch(es)
sp(s)	space/spaces/spaced
st(s)	stitch(es)
tog	together
tr	treble crochet
trtr	triple treble
WS	wrong side
yd(s)	yard(s)
yo	yarn over

Chain—ch: Yo, pull through lp on hook.

Slip stitch—sl st: Insert hook in st, pull through both lps on hook.

Single crochet—sc: Insert hook in st, yo, pull through st, yo, pull through both lps on hook.

Front post stitch—fp: Back post stitch—bp: When working post st, insert hook from right to left around post st on previous row.

Front loop—front lp Back loop—back lp

Front Loop Back Loop

Half double crochet—hdc: Yo, insert hook in st, yo, pull through st, yo, pull through all 3 lps on hook.

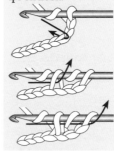

Double crochet—dc: Yo, insert hook in st, yo, pull through st, [yo, pull through 2 lps] twice.

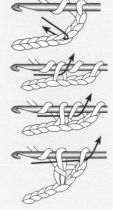

Change colors: Drop first color; with 2nd color, pull through last 2 lps of st.

Treble crochet—tr: Yo twice, insert hook in st, yo, pull through st, [yo, pull through 2 lps] 3 times.

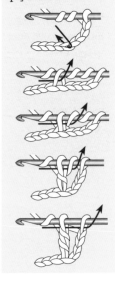

Double treble crochet—dtr: Yo 3 times, insert hook in st, yo, pull through st, [yo, pull through 2 lps] 4 times.

Single crochet decrease (sc dec): (Insert hook, yo, draw lp through) in each of the sts indicated, yo, draw through all lps on hook.

Half double crochet decrease (hdc dec): (Yo, insert hook, yo, draw lp through) in each of the sts indicated, yo, draw through all lps on hook.

Double crochet decrease (dc dec): (Yo, insert hook, yo, draw loop through, draw through 2 lps on hook) in each of the sts indicated, yo, draw through all lps on hook.

Example of 2-tr dec

Treble crochet decrease (tr dec): Holding back last lp of each st, tr in each of the sts indicated, yo, pull through all lps on hook.

US		UK
sl st (slip stitch)	=	sc (single crochet)
sc (single crochet)	=	dc (double crochet)
hdc (half double crochet)	=	htr (half treble crochet)
dc (double crochet)	=	tr (treble crochet)
tr (treble crochet)	=	dtr (double treble crochet)
dtr (double treble crochet)	=	ttr (triple treble crochet)
skip	=	miss

Metric
Conversion
Charts

METRIC CONVERSIONS

yards	x	.9144	=	metres (m)
yards	x	91.44	=	centimetres (cm)
inches	x	2.54	=	centimetres (cm)
inches	x	25.40	=	millimetres (mm)
inches	x	.0254	=	metres (m)

centimetres	x	.3937	=	inches
metres	x	1.0936	=	yards

INCHES INTO MILLIMETRES & CENTIMETRES (Rounded off slightly)

inches	mm	cm	inches	cm	inches	cm	inches	cm
1/8	3	0.3	5	12.5	21	53.5	38	96.5
1/4	6	0.6	5 1/2	14	22	56	39	99
3/8	10	1	6	15	23	58.5	40	101.5
1/2	13	1.3	7	18	24	61	41	104
5/8	15	1.5	8	20.5	25	63.5	42	106.5
3/4	20	2	9	23	26	66	43	109
7/8	22	2.2	10	25.5	27	68.5	44	112
1	25	2.5	11	28	28	71	45	114.5
1 1/4	32	3.2	12	30.5	29	73.5	46	117
1 1/2	38	3.8	13	33	30	76	47	119.5
1 3/4	45	4.5	14	35.5	31	79	48	122
2	50	5	15	38	32	81.5	49	124.5
2 1/2	65	6.5	16	40.5	33	84	50	127
3	75	7.5	17	43	34	86.5		
3 1/2	90	9	18	46	35	89		
4	100	10	19	48.5	36	91.5		
4 1/2	115	11.5	20	51	37	94		

KNITTING NEEDLES CONVERSION CHART

Canada/U.S.	0	1	2	3	4	5	6	7	8	9	10	10½	11	13	15
Metric (mm)	2	2¼	2¾	3¼	3½	3¾	4	4½	5	5½	6	6½	8	9	10

CROCHET HOOKS CONVERSION CHART

Canada/U.S.	1/B	2/C	3/D	4/E	5/F	6/G	8/H	9/I	10/J	10½/K	N
Metric (mm)	2.25	2.75	3.25	3.5	3.75	4.25	5	5.5	6	6.5	9.0

TOLL-FREE ORDER LINE or to request a free catalog (800) LV-ANNIE (800) 582-6643
Customer Service (800) AT-ANNIE (800) 282-6643, **Fax** (800) 882-6643
Visit AnniesAttic.com
We have made every effort to ensure the accuracy and completeness of these instructions.
We cannot, however, be responsible for human error, typographical mistakes or variations in individual work.

ISBN: 978-1-59635-293-3